IMAGES
of England

LEEDS
THE SECOND SELECTION

IMAGES
of England

LEEDS

THE SECOND SELECTION

Vera Chapman

TEMPUS

What you expect – and what you see at Leeds, *c*. 1932.

Frontispiece: Leeds town hall, proud symbol of the town and city.

First published 2002

Tempus Publishing Limited
The Mill, Brimscombe Port,
Stroud, Gloucestershire, GL5 2QG

British Library Cataloguing in Publication Data.
A catalogue record for this book is available from the British Library.

ISBN 0 7524 2650 8

Typesetting and origination by Tempus Publishing Limited
Printed in Great Britain by Midway Colour Print, Wiltshire

Contents

An Edwardian afternoon in Briggate.

Introduction

This book selects several themes which can perhaps be summarised by the postcard on page 4–
'What you expect and what you see at Leeds', busy spacious streets and proud squares, a
profusion of parks, mansions of wealthy entrepreneurs and the household names of firms that
began in Leeds.

Sited strategically in the Aire Gap through the Pennines, Leeds has long been a focal
point for trade and the production of wealth. A new town and market place were created in
the early thirteenth century at the Aire crossing point and those new medieval burgage plots
along Briggate have shaped central Leeds to the present day. As time passed and the effects
of the Industrial Revolution began to be felt, domestic cloth-weaving gave way in turn to
water and steam powered mills along the Aire. Improved river navigation and a new canal
in the eighteenth century allowed better transport of goods. Railways arrived and there
occurred a flowering of the expanding town into a city in late Victorian times. Narrow
medieval streets were transformed into roads lined with commercial buildings of Victorian
grandeur. Old yards along Briggate were into remade into arcades like miniature Crystal
Palaces. The latter half of the nineteenth century saw in Leeds the decline of wool and linen
cloth-making and the diversification into engineering, especially steam traction and railway
engines. There were snags of course, notably smoke pollution and overcrowding, which
fuelled a move outwards into suburbs, but many of the problems have been tackled and the
city now hums with life.

Ready-made clothing, leather boots and shoes, bricks, terracotta and earthenware pottery,
preserves and a diverse range of other goods rose to prominence, some of which also became
household names. Financial services expanded and banks, building societies, insurance and
assurance companies set up with especially fine premises in Park Row.

But why should someone living sixty miles away choose, or presume, to focus on Leeds?
First, I suppose, my family origins are in the West Riding and visits to aunts, uncles,
grandparents and cousins in school holidays and at Christmas were a feature of my
childhood in Manchester. Many cousins' families are still there and my eldest son and family
live and work on the fringe of Leeds.

There are other connections, too. Manchester, Leeds and Darlington all have prominent
buildings designed by Alfred Waterhouse, the leading architect of mid-Victorian England. I
studied at Manchester University in his Owens College building; Owens had a Leeds
connection in the Victoria University of Manchester, Liverpool and Leeds. I was drawn to

the work of historian Maurice Beresford at Leeds University where the original Yorkshire College building was by Waterhouse.

Several things about Leeds also intrigue me: the large number of public statues and their wanderings; the large number of public clocks and the strange Egyptian mill by Bonomi, for example. Yet there are these and other connections between where I now live and Leeds. Cassy Harker, the last hospital Matron in Darlington, trained at Leeds. Flax spinning machinery was invented in Darlington and Marshall of Leeds went on to develop it at Temple Mill. His Durham architect also designed buildings in and around Darlington. John Fowler, the steam traction engine maker, married a Darlington Quaker and Potts, the prolific clockmaker of Leeds, learned his trade in Darlington, both of whom have memorials in my town. So I already had perceptions of Leeds when invited to do this volume. Anyway, I love Victorian towns and was grieved to have to walk past the burning warehouses of Piccadilly, Manchester during the Blitz to get to the safety of West Yorkshire. However, Leeds is still a city of awesome grandeur.

Prospect of Leeds, c. 1715.

One
Along the Aire Valley

Amen Corner, Armley. This quiet scene along the towpath of the Leeds and Liverpool Canal still shows signs of industrial activity. The Yorkshire stretch, begun in 1770, was completed in 1777 and linked with the Aire and Calder Navigation near Leeds Bridge. A link from Shipley to Bradford was made in 1774, but the Lancashire stretch was not completed until 1816.

The Aire from Leeds Bridge, *c.* 1903. Downstream from Leeds Bridge towards the parish church the river, improved as the Aire and Calder Navigation, was lined with wharves, sheds, multistorey warehouses and barges carrying bulk cargoes. Leeds Co-op had its own wharf. This is perhaps a view on a Sunday.

The Aire from Leeds Bridge, 2002. This *is* a Sunday view. It reveals the riverside transformed into an attractive area of renovated warehouses, new buildings, residential flats, restaurants, leisure facilities and Armley Mills Industrial Museum. Thwaite Mills' water-powered grinding mill alongside the Navigation at Hunslet is now a working museum.

Kirkstall Abbey. This painting by an unknown artist was issued by the proprietors of Colman's Starch as an Edwardian postcard. The dramatic ruins of the eleventh-century Cistercian Abbey, dissolved in 1539, stand in parkland beside the Aire four miles upstream from Leeds Bridge. The gatehouse, converted to a dwelling for the last Abbot, is now the Abbey House Museum.

Adel Dam and Adel Mill Farm, c. 1907. About six miles upstream and off the Otley road, this was perhaps a popular place for an Edwardian country walk as the existence of a postcard and the well-made track suggest. The dam impounds a reserve of water at a height to power the mill below. Leeds Country Way now passes close by.

Near Adel Crags. Here was another popular Edwardian destination for a rural ramble, hence the issue of a postcard.

Calverley Cutting, *c.* 1906. This path was a new road cut in around 1850 from Calverley's main road to Apperley Bridge on the Leeds and Liverpool Canal when a residential development in Calverley Woods was proposed. It replaced the old packhorse route from Pudsey which wound, with a gentler gradient and pleasant views, around a hill in the woods. Both roads led to a swing bridge, a wharf for shipping stone, a wool warehouse and a farm.

Seven Arches aqueduct. Near Hirst Farm Lock the Leeds and Liverpool Canal crossed the winding river Aire on a seven-arched aqueduct 30ft high. Here oak and birch woodland reached the canal at a popular beauty spot.

CANAL AT SEVEN ARCHES.

Beside the Canal. Edwardian visitors to Seven Arches and Hirst Farm Woods and Lock are wearing town clothes! At weekends and Bank Holidays the farmer had jugs of tea and home-made cakes for ramblers and visitors. There was ice cream and angling and swimming in the canal.

The river at Saltaire. Better known for Sir Titus Salt's Italianate alpaca wool factory with campanile chimney and his model village across the river and canal, Saltaire also provided a leisure destination with boating on the river. Saltaire showed that industry in a rural setting could be an attractive feature, despite being at the time Europe's largest textile mill.

Japanese Gardens, Saltaire.

Two

Briggate

Briggate and Duncan Street junction. This striking coloured card posted in 1910 shows the characteristic turretted skyline of Leeds' Victorian re-build. It also shows two of the city's great industries: ready-made clothing (Hepworth's advertise on the corner tower) and leather footwear (see left-hand corner) for which Stead and Simpson Ltd were large-scale producers. A large red building is outlined in the background.

Briggate, c. 1904. Taken from Duncan Street junction, some of the shops on the right can be recognised on the previous picture, but the end one was replaced by 1910 by the dramatic new corner building and its tower. The nearer open-topped tram heads for Headingley.

Briggate somewhat later. Spot the changes! The corner, towered building with mock-arched windows has arrived and also a huge brick building with a bracketed clock which proves to be the shadowy outlined building on page 15. On the left are shoes, here revealed as Saxone, with the Cafe Royal above.

Briggate, *c.* 1904. This is a 'flashback'; the large brick building has indeed arrived by this date, but had not gained its clock. The old corner premises were still there, housing a sixpence-halfpenny bazaar and Ford's (Ladies' Mantles).

Briggate. Duncan Street junction is this time pictured from ground level. The new buildings tower above the few remains of the old market street. Turrets and pinnacles have become a constant celebration of Leeds' prosperity.

Briggate, *c*. 1910. The east side of upper Briggate north of Kirkgate and through to Vicar Lane was redeveloped by the Leeds Estate Company when in 1897 the City Council widened Vicar Lane and opened up Queen Victoria Street and King Edward Street. The company built the Empire Palace Theatre as part of the County Arcade and Cross Arcade scheme designed by Frank Matcham and completed in 1903.

Briggate, *c*. 1906. The twin turrets and corner wall-clock (mid-right) mark the Briggate entrance to King Edward Street. The Buck Vaults on the right end this comprehensive redevelopment in the red brick and buff terracotta style fashionable at the turn of the century. (See also pages 59 and 60)

The Empire Palace. This theatre, with its ornate frontage, catered for popular entertainment. Great music hall stars performed here, as did the escape artist Houdini. It closed in 1961 with a pantomime *Babes in the Wood*, and became the Empire Arcade. The Grand Theatre and Opera House in New Briggate, seating about 2,500, catered for a more serious clientele.

Corner Turrets, King Edward Street, 2002. This street remains open, whereas its parallel companion Queen Victoria Street has been glazed over as a shopping arcade, the Victoria Quarter. (Vera Chapman)

Briggate, c. 1910. Gas lamps, electric trams and horse-drawn traffic mingle. One of Leeds' astonishing number of unmissable public clocks on brackets and towers is prominent on the right. How many clocks can you count in this book? (See pages 79-80)

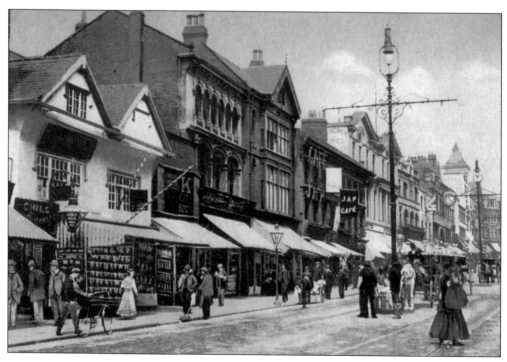

Briggate. Newer buildings on the left have an Edwardian Art Nouveau flavour. The horse-drawn cabs still line up along the centre, and, yes, there's a clock!

Three
City Square

In 1893 Queen Victoria granted City Status to Leeds. At the time, the Council was creating a new square where Quebec Street, Wellington Street, Infirmary Street, Park Row and Boar Lane converged. It was felt that it would be a more fitting approach for the growing number of visitors arriving by train at Wellington Street Station. So it was proudly named City Square and the station renamed City Station.

The Coloured Cloth Hall, *c*. 1905. The hall had been built in 1785 in the days of Leeds' preeminence in the manufacture and merchanting of woollen cloth. Having fallen into disuse it was demolished in 1890, the entrance gateway on the left alone being preserved. The new GPO was built on the site.

Quebec Buildings. These buildings adjacent to the old Cloth Hall, also in a poor state, were demolished when creating the new City Square.

New Square and statuary. The Black Prince was a symbol of chivalry and democracy. Eight draped maidens as Morn and Even brandish electric torches. Dr Hook, vicar, James Watt, pioneer of steam power, John Harrison, philanthropist and Joseph Priestley, minister and 'discoverer' of oxygen stand in the four corner gardens. (See page 105)

General Post Office. This new Renaissance-style building on the site of the old Coloured Cloth Hall was designed by Henry Tanner of HM Board of Works and opened in 1896. Its clock turret and lantern, twin chimneys and granite pillars are striking features. Wings in Quebec Street and Infirmary Street enclose a rear-covered yard for despatching mail.

Queen's Hotel by William Perkins, opened in 1863 was replaced in 1973 by a modern white block. The domed building with tall columns at the end of Boar Lane by W.W. Gwyther opened as the Yorkshire Banking Company's HQ. Statues on the parapet of corn, sickle, sheep and plough represent the bank's agricultural interest. It became the Observatory pub and then a restaurant.

The Standard Life Assurance Building, built in 1902. One of the four corner gardens and a statue appear on the left. The trees and statuary soon suffered from the smoke then prevalent. A century later restoration and re-organisation of the Square are now in progress.

Four

Park Row, Vicar Lane Commercial Street, and Boar Lane

Park Row and City Square, Leeds.   E. Bishop, Leeds.

Park Row from City Square, c. 1921, a handsome business street with buildings of Victorian solidity. The prominent Standard Life Building of 1902, designed by Archibald Neille of Leeds, housed fifty suites of offices, banks and insurance companies, a City Club and the City Tramway Company. On the right is Priestley Hall by Crowther, which housed Mill Hill Chapel Schools.

Park Row, c. 1908. Posted in that year, the message reads 'A reminder from Leeds. Great Place.' Beckett's Bank on the right, one of the more ornate ones, was designed as early Gothic in red brick with stone dressings and marble shafts by George Gilbert Scott.

Park Row, Leeds.

Park Row. On the right is the Court House designed by Thomas Taylor and built in 1811-13. Park Row is lit by gas lamps. On the left, the porch over the pavement and the vases on the roof balustrade identify the Philosophical Society's building.

Park Row. This similar closer view of the Court House shows up its splendid cast iron railings. The vista along Park Row ended dramatically with the Roman Catholic cathedral. This was eventually demolished in 1899 as a traffic problem, and the statue of Sir Robert Peel MP was removed for the same reason.

Park Row, c. 1904. The message sent to Glasgow was: 'A glorious day and a fine city.' In Park Row were also the Commercial Union Bank and the delightfully-named Hand in Hand Insurance Company. Lloyds Bank 1898 and the Prudential Assurance Company building of 1894 were both designed in brick and terracotta by Alfred Waterhouse. The Royal Insurance Company building, too, was early Waterhouse.

Park Row, *c.* 1904. the message sent to glasgow was 'A glorious day and a fine city'. In Park row were also the Commercial Union Bank and the delightfully named Hand in Hand Insurance Company. Lloyds Bank, built 1898 and the Prudential Assurance Company building of 1894 were both designed in brick and terracotta by Alfred Waterhouse. The Royal Insurance company building, too, was early Waterhouse.

Commercial Street, *c.* 1907. Here the narrow street and styles of buildings have a flavour of Georgian Leeds. Men's suits on the left are opposite Moffat's Ladies Modes on the right. On the corner of Commercial Street and Albion Street was 'the finest office palazzo in Leeds'.

Kirkgate and Commercial Street. As we look in the opposite direction the spirelet is seen again, and a tram is crossing. Note the early high-backed motor car on the left. There is an early Macdonalds on the left, too! The tram advertises tomato soup.

Vicar Lane. In 1897, having been designated a city in 1893, Leeds City Council widened Vicar Lane threefold. New warehouses, offices and shops were then built with characteristic turrets and dormers.

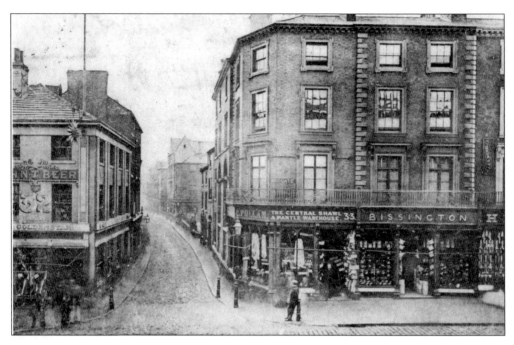

Boar Lane Corner, *c.* 1860. Features of medieval and Georgian Leeds are recorded here in Mr Bissington's advertising card. A hatter, hosier, shirtmaker and gentlemen's outfitter at 34 Briggate, he writes apologies to a Roundhay customer for not delivering a hat as the lad could not find the house: 'We will send tomorrow.'

Boar Lane, *c.* 1905. Flanking the Park Row and City Square end are the domed Yorkshire Banking Company building and the ornate Gothic Royal Exchange and its clock tower. Statuettes of local historical worthies once graced its traceried parapet.

Boar Lane. In 1868 it was trebled in width and then mostly rebuilt with stately warehouses and shops, becoming, with Briggate, one of Leeds' two main shopping streets. The Wrenish tower and steeple of Holy Trinity church (1721 and 1841) soar aloft.

Boar Lane, c. 1907. Details of the impressive streetscape are here shown alongside Holy Trinity church.

Boar Lane, *c.* 1921. The Pygmalion Great Summer Sale is being advertised on the left, Leeds' first department store. Jones, Schweppes and Singer are well-known trade names.

Boar Lane. Waterproofs, costumes and mantles are advertised and 'highest class dentistry' by a London dentist.

Boar Lane. The street retains its ancient curve despite Victorian improvement. A variety of traffic shares the carriageway.

Boar Lane. Beyond its junction with Briggate, Boar Lane becomes Duncan Street to the mighty Corn Exchange.

Ancient Bell Pit. Much of central Leeds was riddled with medieval bell pits, shallow workings which mined an ironstone seam, but usually left the adjacent coal seam untouched. This was one of the pits cleared away to provide firm foundations for the Victory Hotel near Briggate. (P.F. Kendall and H.E. Wroot, *The Geology of Yorkshire*, Vol. 1, 1924)

which leads

33

.ight.

Five

Suburbs & Outskirts

Harrogate Road, Moortown. In Victorian and Edwardian times villas in gardens were built on the higher ground north of the smoky industrial zone near the river, canal and old town centre.

Spencer Place. Substantial stone terraces like this between Harehills Avenue and Roundhay Road, near Sheepscar, took the middle ground. Elegance was added by tree-planting on grass verges. Did the name have a Marks and Spencer connection?

Three Horse Shoes, c. 1911. Doubtless the name of the pub in the distance.

Pudsey, c. 1914. Once part of Calverley parish, Pudsey gained its parish church of St Laurence in 1821. Its once-busy Lowtown and Greenside railway stations on the Great Northern line from Leeds Central station were closed in 1964. Pudsey formerly had twenty-two woollen mills and was the birthplace of the famous cricketers Herbert Sutcliffe, Ray Illingworth and Sir Leonard (Len) Hutton.

Armley, Branch Road. This photograph by J.F. Lawrence includes industrial buildings near the Aire and a few of the mill chimneys which were formerly such a feature.

Shire Oak, Headingley, pre-1909. This venerable oak reputedly existed from Saxon times and gave its name to Skyrack (Scire Oak) Wapentake. Traditionally it was a Saxon leaders' meeting place and even a Roman signal station!

Shire Oak, now a mere shell with a weird shape. This massive remnant was latterly protected by the low wall and railings. Tram passengers to Headingley would know it.

Skyrack Inn. Named after the old oak locally regarded with affection, the tree suddenly collapsed in 1941. Note the setts in the foreground typical of Leeds streets and roads.

Setts. Leeds Council Highways Department from 1869 until 1884 opened up and quarried the igneous Cleveland dyke at Great Ayton to provide setts, kerbstones and cart-tracks. The tough grey basalt-like whinstone had been intruded like an underground wall 40-80ft wide from its origin in a volcanic episode in the Hebrides in Tertiary times.

Cliff Rigg and Langbaurgh Quarries. Opened when a railway arrived and long abandoned, the quarries left a great linear gash or gorge after mining in ranks of parallel tunnels and quarrying at the surface.

Setts near the White Cloth Hall, Call Lane, Leeds. Setts were hand-shaped with hammers by sett-dressers using a heavy, square-ended cavil, then a smaller knapper. Note the irregular edges.

Six
Architectural Landmarks

Leeds Town hall. This magnificent building reflects the wealth, importance and prosperity of Victorian Leeds. Designed by the young architect Cuthbert Brodrick and opened by Queen Victoria in 1858, it is here seen before smoke blackened the stone.

Victoria Hall. At the heart of the Town Hall is the barrel vaulted civic and concert hall, the roof supported by a double row of coupled columns. The vast organ by a London designer fills the apsidal end. The hall was the main venue for classical concerts and music festivals. The steeply-raked seating was for choirs. Brodrick also designed the chandeliers. The entrance hall displays statuary and much marble.

Leeds Corn Exchange, c. 1905. Call Lane leads under the railway to Brodrick's oval Corn Exchange of 1860-63, 'one of the great works of Victorian architecture'. Severe yet beautiful, a symphony of arches and a triumph of design matched to function, it was revealed to view by the later nineteenth century widening of Duncan Street. The domed roof, glazed at the top and north curve, was carried over a vast unimpeded floor space for displaying samples, surrounded by two floors of merchants' offices. In 1990 it was sensitively converted to a shopping centre.

Leeds Institute of Science, Art and Literature, *c.* 1905. Cuthbert Brodrick's building of 1865-68 housed the Mechanics Institute founded in 1824. Its heavy design was said to intimidate the workmen it was intended to educate! Its central circular lecture hall and gallery seated 1,400, surrounded by classrooms for art, design, music and technical schools, laboratories and workshops for around 1,500 students. It is now the Civic Theatre.

Leeds Institute. This picture gives clearer details of Brodrick's Institute faced in hard local stone. In Leeds he also designed the City Baths, Headingley Hill Congregational chapel (now offices) and other non-conformist chapels and several large warehouses and offices, as well as the major buildings illustrated in this section. Hull-born, he designed Hull Town Hall and Royal Institution and in Withernsea the Royal Hotel. He died in 1905.

Wells House, Ilkley, *c.* 1900. Of palatial design and proportions, Brodrick's hydropathic hotel, Wells House, 1853-58, high on the moor edge above the small spa town, faced into a central open court around which a spacious heated perimeter corridor enabled indoor exercise in poor weather. The cupolas on the corner towers were later removed. From the terrace with its spectacular views, landscaped gardens and steps led to a marble bath and covered terrace. (See page 119)

Grand Hotel, Scarborough. Perched high on St Nicholas' cliff overlooking South Bay and the Spa, Brodrick's spectacularly-sited hotel of monumental proportions, built 1862-67, dominates the seafront with its dormers and domes, its serried ranks of arched windows and more than thirteen storeys in yellow brick and red sandstone. Its grand staircase, lounge and 365 bedrooms gave a luxury and magnificence eagerly patronised by the wealthy of Leeds and the West Riding. (see page 123)

Leeds Civic Hall. This fine new administrative building, designed by Vincent Harris, was opened in 1933. Its twin Wren-like towers are each topped by an owl, part of the city coat of arms and an official symbol of Leeds. It was funded by the City Council using grants to create work for the unemployed during the Great Depression.

Civic Hall Courtyard. The Civic Hall is now becoming part of Leeds Millennium Square, surrounded by the Town Hall, General Infirmary (page 52) and the Civic Theatre (page 43) with refurbishment as restaurants and apartments and renamed Brodrick's Court. The square will feature civic ceremonies and public events and entertainment. A water feature, sculptures and a temporary winter ice-skating rink are planned.

General Post Office, City Square, *c*. 1903. Designed in Renaissance style by Henry Tanner of HM Board of Works, the new GPO on the site of the old Coloured Cloth Hall was opened in 1896. With its Renaissance-style facade, granite pillars and clock tower with lantern, it dominated that side of City Square. Wings on Quebec Street and Infirmary Street enclosed a covered yard for despatching mail.

GPO and Standard Life Assurance Buildings. The latter, completed in 1902 in stone in classic style, was designed by Archibald Neill of Leeds. It presented a bright, solid seven-storey front to City Square between Infirmary Street and Park Row and was one of the city's most prominent buildings.

City Markets. Located for some 600 years in Briggate, Leeds' market for animals, vegetables and fruit moved in 1922 to Vicar's Croft between Kirkgate and Vicar Lane. By 1857 a cast iron and glass hall like a plain version of the famous Crystal Palace in London was built and Briggate Market finally ceased.

City Markets. In 1901-04 the present building designed by Leeming & Leeming took its place in ornate Flemish style with a stone exterior and a cast iron interior with a perimeter gallery and a huge glass roof. Bombed in the Second World War and damaged by fire in 1975, it is restored and has about 750 stalls. In 1984, Marks & Spencer presented the clock under the central dome to mark the centenary of Michael Marks' Penny Bazaar on that site.

Leeds Industrial Co-operative Society. This Co-operative Society was founded in 1847, commencing in Benyon's flax mill. At a time when Leeds was growing rapidly and diversifying from its traditional industries, it became one of the country's largest Co-operative Societies. It owned shops, factories, farms, flour mills and its canal-side wharf in Leeds city centre.

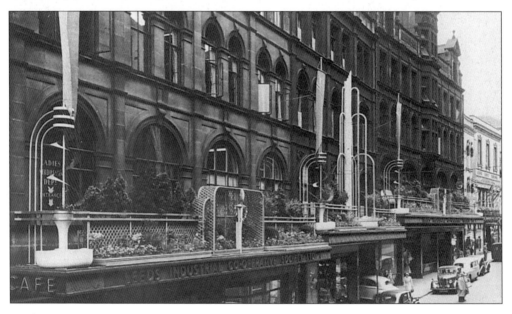

Leeds Co-op's Albion Street Premises. The foundation stone of its handsome and extensive premises in Albion Street were laid in 1883. They included a public meeting and assembly room on an upper floor known as the People's Hall. By the early 1900s it had nearly 50,000 members. (These Leeds Co-op photographs are courtesy of Mr Alan Gill, Chief Executive, Leeds Co-operative Society Ltd, Benyon House, Leeds).

Leeds Co-operative Society, Chemists and Photographic Department, Albion Street.

Leeds Co-operative Society, Pharmacy and Dispensary, Albion Street. This prestigious street also housed the Yorkshire Post (an Alfred Waterhouse building), the Leeds and Yorkshire Assurance Company's 'palazzo' and a mixture of merchants in oysters, sugar, ostrich feather dyeing, music, jelly-making and flag-quarrying!

Leeds Co-operative Society, 1917, Directors and Officials. Front row, from left to right: A. Morgan, W. Argile, W. Cockshaw, J. Smith (President), Briggs (Secretary), W. Whitworth. The lady is Mrs C.P. Stainer.

Leeds Co-operative Society, 1947, Heads of Departments and Managers. Departments represented are: furnishing, restaurant, pharmacy, jewellery, butchering, drapery, tinners, bakery, grocery stores, grocery, building, tailoring, laundry, electric, greengrocery, flour mill, boot and shoe, traffic, coal, wheelwright and dairy.

Grand Theatre and Opera House. Designed by George Corson and opened in 1878, its Gothic exterior sheltered a sumptuous interior in an Italianate style with ornamental plasterwork. Its fan-vaulted, domed and many-tiered auditorium was decorated in crimson and gold. It catered for drama and culture and could seat over 3,000. There were assembly and supper rooms and its frontage has shops and offices. Northern Ballet and Opera North now perform here.

Ceylon Café, c. 1905. The postcard message was 'This café is fine. There is a band and a fountain playing. We went in here today.'

Leeds General Infirmary. In Great George Street at Calverley Street corner and near St George's church, the infirmary was built in 1863-68 to the design of Sir George Gilbert Scott RA. It was built in the Gothic style using the then fashionable red and black polychrome bricks and stone dressings. Arranged on the pavilion plan, each ward was isolated, as recommended by Florence Nightingale, to prevent the spread of infection.

Leeds General Infirmary. In 1891-92, George Corson, the leading local Gothic architect, added the identical east pavilion. The infirmary is now part of the Civic Hall area redevelopment into Millennium Square, bringing together the finest public buildings of the city old and new.

Hospital for Women and children , Springfield Lodge. This hospital was established in 1853 in East Parade. It moved to Springfield Lodge, Woodbine Place, Little Woodhouse Street in 1861-62, and was extended in 1902-03 with an entrance in Coventry Place. It was supported by voluntary subscriptions.

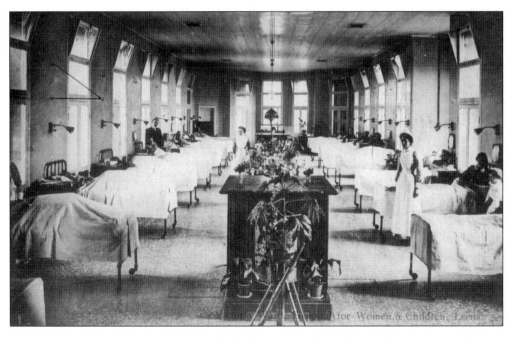

Victoria Ward, Hospital for Women and Children. Note the well-spaced beds and windows in this pavilion-style wing, similar to those of the General Infirmary, and the uniforms of the two nurses. (see page 81)

The Yorkshire College, *c.* 1904. The College opened in 1874 for education in science and technical subjects useful in manufacturing, mining, engineering and agriculture. The original college buildings were begun in 1877 by Alfred Waterhouse. Soon arts subjects and textiles were added and in 1887 with the School of Medicine, it became part of the Victoria University of Manchester, Liverpool and Leeds. In 1904 it became independent as the University of Leeds.

The Yorkshire College, *c.* 1902. Waterhouse's buildings were extended several times in the 1890s and early 1900s in the Waterhousean Prudential Assurance style in red brick. The Brotherton Library was added in 1936 and the Parkinson building in 1950.

The Old Grammar School interior. This was built on a new site by John Harrison, philanthropist, in 1624, housing a school with origins in the previous century. It ceased as a school in 1859, when the school moved to a new building in Clarendon Road designed by E.M. Barry. The old building was demolished in 1894.

New Technical School, Pudsey, c. 1914. Is this now Pudsey Grangefield School in Richardshaw Lane?

Cavendish Hall Training College. This college for training women teachers opened in Beckett Park in 1912, the former grounds of William Beckett, banker and MP for Leeds 1841-52. Situated north-west of the city near Headingley, Weetwood and Kirkstall Abbey, it became successively the City of Leeds Training College, Leeds Polytechnic and the Metropolitan University of Leeds.

Headingley College, *c.* 1904.

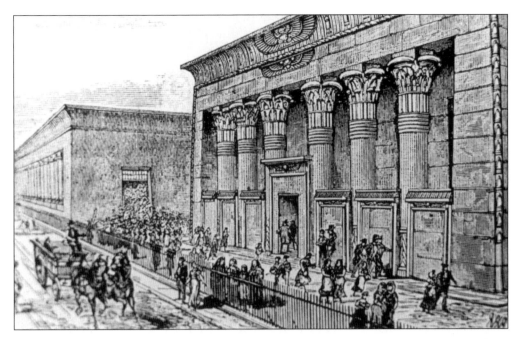

Marshall's Temple Mills, Holbeck, Leeds. Temple Mill, 1838-40, was designed by the Durham architect Ignatius Bonomi in the Egyptian style popular after Napoleon's Egyptian campaign of 1798. The office is stone-fronted with giant lotus leaf columns. The plainer building on the left is the mill. Water power gave way to steam, but the obelisk-shaped mill chimney has gone.

Marshall's Flax Mill Interior. A machine for spinning flax, a tough irregular fibre, was patented in 1787 by John Kendrew and Thomas Porthouse of Darlington, who set up two water-driven flax-spinning mills on the river Skerne for shoe thread. John Marshall apparently improved the process and prospered, and was unsuccessfully sued for patent infringement. The mill roof is supported by iron columns, and sixty-six glazed domes gave daylight for the looms. Under-floor central heating was provided.

Thornton's Arcade, Briggate, 2002. Shopping arcades are a feature of Briggate. Old burgage plots or yards behind the town's original street have been roofed over. Thornton's in 1877 was the first, Queens's in 1888 the second.

County Arcade, 2002. This sumptuous arcade, dated 1900, with Cross Arcade at right angles to it was part of the Leeds Estate Company's redevelopment of the area between Vicar Lane and Briggate from 1898-1903 and also of building the Empire Theatre.

County Arcade. Details of the moulded designs reveal the scope of terracotta, burnt clay unglazed.

County Arcade. Its facade on Briggate is a triumphant display of red and orange terracotta.

Jubilee Hotel. Dated 1897, it faces the Town Hall. Victoria Square is now the Headrow. The main doorway is on its corner.

Jubilee Hotel. The side doorway is flat, the main doorway on the corner curved and more elaborate in its moulded patterns.

Seven

Churches

Leeds Old Parish Church. The fourteenth century church of St Peter in Kirkgate, one of the largest in the West Riding, served a vast parish. It replaced a church destroyed by fire. Its size reflected the growing importance of Leeds, its tower a landmark. Demolition in 1838 revealed a smashed Anglo-Saxon cross.

Leeds New Parish Church. The present church was built for Dr W.F. Hook, a reforming vicar, 1837-59, with High Church leanings and an energetic builder of new churches, schools and vicarages. Designed by R.D. Chantrell in Perpendicular Gothic, it was built in Bramley Fell stone quarried at Horsforth.

Parish Church Interior. It seats up to 2,000 with highly ornamental galleries on three sides, and has memorials to Sir John Beckett, banker, William Beckett MP and banker, Benjamin Gott, industrialist and Dr Hook, vicar. The pre-Conquest cross has been restored.

St John's, New Briggate, pre-1919. Built by the cloth merchant and philanthropist John Harrison in 1638, it is a rare example of a church built in Stuart times. Intervention by George Gilbert Scott averted demolition.

St John's church interior. Its nave and one aisle are of the same size. An unwise restoration in the 1860s was slowly reversed and the screens and pulpit reconstructed. In the founder's chapel, John Harrison's good works are depicted in stained glass.

St. Ann's Church,
Leeds.

The old Roman Catholic church and Cathedral of St Anne. This former landmark at the end of Park Row (see part Four) was demolished in 1899 as part of a Leeds Corporation's city improvement scheme (see page 70). St Anne's, named for Anne Humble, a late Sister of Grace and a benefactor, was designed by a local architect John Child and built in 1838. Cathedral status was conferred in 1878 for the new Roman Catholic Diocese of Leeds.

64

St Aidan's Church, Roundhay Road. This vast church in red brick with stone dressings is in Italian Romanesque style with an apsidal baptistery at the west end and two turrets, two aisles, a high clerestory and massive nave pillars. It seats 2000 and was built in 1891-94 by R.J. Johnson and A. Crawford-Hick as a Bishop Woodford memorial.

The high Altar of red Mansfield stone in the apsidal chancel is reached by a central flight of sixteen steps. A rood screen or beam and crucifixion was added in 1898. St Aidan's is famous for its Ravenna-like mosaics by Sir Frank Brangwyn which, in a semi-circle round the altar, tell the story of St Aidan with a procession of people waiting to be baptised by him. The pulpit and font are of various marbles.

Mill Hill Chapel, City Square. This elegant Perpendicular Gothic building on the right was designed by Bowman & Crowther in 1848 to replace the original Presbyterian chapel of 1672. There is no tower or steeple and the main door is in the side centre. It is now Unitarian. Dr Joseph Priestley FRS, 'discoverer' of oxygen, was the minister here from 1767-1773.

Kirkstall Abbey from the south-east. On the north bank of the Aire the ruins of the Cistercian Abbey built around 1175 are the most substantial and tallest remains of any of this Order in England. It was built from the adjacent outcrop of Millstone Grit which later developed as Bramley Fall, Park and Park Spring Quarries. These yielded some of the best and most durable stone in the UK so it is no wonder this abbey lasted so well. Built rapidly, it remained unaltered until the Dissolution, housing monks from Fountains Abbey.

Kirkstall Abbey from the north-west. The west front shows here to advantage, with its ceremonial west door and two large round-headed windows above. The abbey has numerous round-headed openings for windows and doorways, but structural arches are pointed.

Kirkstall Abbey Nave. Here we look down the nave past complex piers and Gothic arches and under the lofty crossing tower arches to the great east window. Lack of ornamentation complied with the intentions of the Order for simplicity. The upper part of the tower, raised in the sixteenth century, collapsed in 1779. In 1889 the Abbey and grounds were bought by Colonel John North and donated to the city.

Moortown church. One of several built after the First World War as the suburbs expanded, especially on to the higher ground to the north around Headingley, Weetwood, Moortown and Roundhay for example.

St John the Baptist church, Adel, *c.* 1905. Adel is a little farther west from Moortown and still on the edge of the built-up area today, but settlement here is ancient, as witnessed by this precious little church. The artist's painting by 'Rambler' gives it a romantic aspect.

Adel church, *c.* 1904. Pevsner described it as 'One of the best and most complete Norman village churches in Yorkshire'. Its zigzag and other ornamentation is superb.

Overleaf: New Roman Catholic Cathedral of St Anne. The former cathedral (see page 64) was bought and demolished by Leeds Corporation in 1899 and the new St Anne's built on a nearby city-centre site offered by the Corporation at the junction of Cookridge Street and Great George Street. The Leeds-born London architect J.H. Eastwood, assisted by S.K. Greenslade, designed their Arts and Crafts Gothic church to fit the limited site yet manage to give a spacious impression. The presbytery built around 1904 in Great George Street is of similar style. The Lady Chapel altar (1842 by Pugin) and pulpit (*c.* 1865) came from the previous church.

Eight
Statues and Portraits

Queen Anne and the Moot Hall. Briggate was the original street and market place of the medieval new town of Leeds. The town's administrative Moot Hall of 1615 at Middle Row was rebuilt in 1710-11 with a Court Room above open shambles (butchers' stalls). The white marble statue of Queen Anne, who reigned 1702-1714, was placed in a niche in 1713 but removed in 1825 to the old Corn Exchange when the Moot Hall was demolished as a traffic obstruction. Later it went to the Town Hall and then to the Art Gallery.

Prudentia. A statue of Prudence was placed as a symbol on all Prudential Assurance Company's buildings. The architect to 'the Pru' was Alfred Waterhouse, who designed the company's corporate house-style in hot red brick and terracotta. Leeds' Pru was built in Park Row in 1894. (Photograph courtesy of Mike Hein-Hartmann)

Queen Victoria Memorial, 1906, by George J. Frampton. It is flanked by figures of Peace and Industry and the Queen bears an orb and sceptre. The base figures represent the four Dominions: Africa, India, Canada and Australia. The statues of Queen Victoria, and also of Sir Robert Peel, the Duke of Wellington and Edward Baines MP, were removed from Victoria Square to Woodhouse Moor when the Square was re-organised.

Edward, the Black Prince. This statue was presented by Colonel T. Walter Harding in 1903 as the centrepiece for the new City Square. The Prince had no direct connection with Leeds except perhaps to reflect the ideals of chivalry and peoples' rights. The two panels represent the battles of Crecy and a sea battle at Sluys. Over 100,000 attended the formal presentation ceremony. (page 105)

Morn or Even? Bearing electric torch lamps, scantily-dressed art nouveau maidens representing Morn and Eve (four of each) perch on the circular balustrade of City Square. Statues of James Watt (steam power), Joseph Priestley (oxygen), John Harrison (philanthropy) and Walter Farquhar Hook (church development) celebrate men of local significance.

John Harrison (1579-1656). A cloth merchant in Briggate and a philanthropist, he used his great wealth for charitable projects. With others he bought Leeds' manorial rights from the Crown. He owned a large area to the north of the town, and built and endowed St John's Church (page 63), a hospital for poor people and a new grammar school. His tomb is in the church he founded, his statue is in City Square and his name is in Harrison Street.

Dr Joseph Priestley (1733-1804). A theologian, writer, eminent scientist and the son of a Yorkshire cloth dresser, Priestley was the Presbyterian minister of Mill Hill Chapel from 1767-1773. At Chippenham in 1774 Dr Priestley independently discovered oxygen in his laboratory at Bowood House under the patronage of the first Lord Lansdowne.

Dr Walter Farqhuar Hook (Vicar of Leeds 1837-1859) When he arrived, Leeds was a centre of Non-Conformists and chapel-building. The old St Peter's had rotting foundations. He was a dynamic organiser and preacher. St Peter's was rebuilt (pages 61 and 62), Dr Hook raising funds for this. He created smaller parishes with new churches, schools and parsonages to a total of twenty-five new churches and day schools. When he left, Leeds had thirty-six Anglican churches.

Edward Baines MP (1774-1848). Born in Lancashire, Baines came to Leeds in 1795, a poor journeyman printer. With help he bought the *Leeds Mercury* and later became its editor. A Liberal and sometime Leeds MP he was a powerful influence with a practical interest in popular education. He was the chief founder and first president of the Mechanics Institute. Edward Baines, Benjamin Gott and John Marshall are said to have been the leading manufacturing and intellectual minds of Leeds for half a century and the authors of much of Leeds' late Victorian prosperity. Baines' statue is in the Town Hall.

Joseph Hepworth JP.
J. Hepworth & Son were wholesale clothiers in a factory rebuilt and enlarged around 1888 to six storeys and twelve bays length with rows of Gothic windows. The display windows were on the Wellington Street front, off City Square. When Bradford and Halifax overtook Leeds in woollen cloth-making, Leeds developed ready-made clothing, and leather was developed for boot and shoe making, for example by Stead and Simpson. Hepworth was Lord Mayor in 1906.

John Fowler (1826-1864) With Albert Fry he experimented and made the mole drainage plough in 1850. His steam cultivator won the 1858 prize of the Royal Agricultural Society. This he improved in 1860 by his invention of the double engine tackle. He took out thirty-two patents for himself and partners during 1850-64, and steam traction became one of Leeds' largest industries. A Quaker, he married Lucy, youngest child of Joseph Pease MP of the Darlington dynasty of industrial entrepreneurs, and died young from a hunting accident. (Portrait courtesy of Darlington Public Library)

Fowler Steam Roller, Funchal, Madeira. This Fowler engine is preserved in the public park in Funchal next to the President's house and grounds. (Photograph by Vera Chapman)

Plaque on the Fowler Engine, Funchal. (Photograph by Vera Chapman)

Fowler Multiple Ploughing Machine. This example was displayed at the Pickering steam traction engine rally around 1964. Note the rope-winding drum. In 1860 John Fowler, a civil engineer, founded the Fowler Engine Works at Leeds. It became one of Leeds' major industries. (Photograph by Vera Chapman)

John Fowler 1856. Memorial, formerly in South Park, Darlington

John Fowler 1856 Memorial. The model of the three-furrow balance plough shows the reversible multiple ploughshares activated by a pair of engines, one at each end of a field. It was ideal for cultivating heavy soils. 1856 was the year in which the first set was built.

Potts Memorial Clock, *c.* 1907. An extra storey for a Potts clock was added to the tower in Darlington's South Park to commemorate William Potts (1809-1887) the clockmaker. Like his father, he trained as a clockmaker in Darlington. From 1832 he set up in Leeds and developed a thriving business making large clocks for the towers of factories, churches and public buildings and for railway companies. He became the official clockmaker to the Great Northern, Midland and North Eastern Railways. He was buried at Pudsey.

William Potts Plaque above Park House Doorway.

The Potts Memorial today.

Maurice W. Beresford (1920-) Maurice Beresford became Lecturer in Economic History at the University of Leeds in 1948 and in 1959 its first Professor in that subject. From the 1950s his books were published: *The Lost Villages of England, History on the Ground, Medieval England: an Aerial Survey* (with J.K.S St Joseph), *New Towns of the Middle Ages* and (with G.R. Jones) *Leeds and its Region*. In 1962 I photographed him perched on the parish churchyard wall, expounding the curious histories of Old and New Thirsk.

Probationer Nurses at Leeds General Infirmary, *c.* 1932. Cassy M. Harker (right) of Barnard Castle began her career at LGI aged nineteen when nursing meant an unmarried cloistered life in the Nurses' Home, receiving not pay but an 'allowance' for three or four years and making one's own uniforms. On the left is Elsie Thorn. (Photograph courtesy of the late Miss Harker)

Cassy M. Harker (1912-1996). During the Second World War, Miss Harker was back at Leeds as Ward Sister and Theatre Sister coping with bomb casualties. Later Matron at Chester, then at Northallerton and Darlington, she retired in 1974, possibly the last Matron in the NHS. Her autobiography is entitled *Call Me Matron*. (Photograph courtesy of the late Miss Harker)

Eric Harrison (1918- ?). A schoolboy prodigy, solo pianist and organist, Eric performed widely in the West Riding. He became Professor of Piano at the Royal College of Music 1947-60 and broadcast for the BBC. From 1960 he was Senior Lecturer in Piano in Melbourne University, Australia. My grandparents and his were friends. Here are Eric and I at Sunny Vale, Hipperholme, *c.* 1930.

Nine
Mansions, Parks & Gardens

Temple Newsam. This Tudor-Jacobean house was first built by Thomas Lord Darcy in Henry VIII's reign and bought in 1622 by a London merchant, Sir Arthur Ingram, who extended it until around 1630. After 300 years of the Ingrams, it was bought in 1922 by Leeds Corporation to display art treasures and period furniture. Around 1000 acres of the grounds were landscaped by Capability Brown. (F.O. Morris, *Picturesque Views*, Vol. I, D. Banks, Leeds)

Harewood House. In 1738 Henry Lascelles bought the Harewood and Gawthorpe estates of the Gascoigne family. His son Lord Harewood demolished Gawthorpe House and in 1759-65 built this new house designed by John Carr of York who also designed the stables, farm buildings and the model village at the main gate. In the 1760s came Robert Adam's sumptuous interiors. Capability Brown enlarged the lake and landscaped the park, and Sir Charles Barry added the terrace with parterres and fountains. Girtin and Turner painted here. (*Picturesque Views*, Vol. I op.cit.)

Harewood Castle. The gaunt ruins of the fourteenth century castle, itself superseded by Gawthorpe Hall, can be glimpsed from the Leeds-Harrogate Road and the village. There are remnants of the Great Hall, kitchen, vaulted basement, solar and chapel.

Calverley Old Hall. This medieval manor house by the A657 in Calverley village was for over 500 years the seat of the Calverley family who were usually knights or baronets. From 1190, their records were kept here in a chest, a rare and complete collection now in the British Library. The house was sold in 1754 to Thomas Thornhill and divided into nine cottages, but remained otherwise intact with its solar, great hall, chapel and later north wing. (Photographs courtesy of The Landmark Trust)

Calverley Hall Chapel. The Trust saves, restores and cares for historic buildings and lets as holiday cottages to discerning visitors. The chapel and the massive timbers of the great hall roof are now repaired and a detailed house history is being researched. The solar wing is thirteenth century. The chapel is almost unique with its small-scale hammerbeam roof and private family gallery.

Kirkstall Abbey Park. The grounds of the abbey bordering on the Aire are now one of Leeds' many municipal parks, bought by Colonel North for the town in 1888. The abbey gatehouse where the abbot lived after the dissolution is now Kirkstall Abbey museum, where streets of Victorian workers' houses and shops have been reconstructed.

Mansion House, Roundhay Park, c. 1907. London banker Thomas Nicholson's early nineteenth-century mansion stands in a former deer park that is around 900 years old, bought in 1803 for development. On one side, villas with large gardens were planned and on the other a mansion and country estate with a carriage drive from the Leeds-Wetherby road. The mansion later became a school, then a hotel.

Roundhay Park, Upper Terrace, c. 1906. Nicholson's mansion of 1826 commanded extensive views from a central high point in his park. It was bought by Leeds Corporation in 1872 and opened that year as a 700 acre municipal park by HRH Prince Arthur. A golf course and swimming, boating and sports facilities developed later. The arrival of tram transport enabled mass public access to what was described at the turn of the century as 'the finest provincial park in England'.

The Formal Walk, Roundhay Park. This led down past the fountain basin to more park seats.

A view from the terrace. The ornamental fountain is at play where the urns and steps mark a change of gradient. The walk leads to the bandstand and lake in the left distance.

Drinking Fountain rotunda, erected in 1882. In the foreground a man is drawing water at an arched bowl and tap.

Canal Garden with Swan, *c.* 1907. Beyond the sheltering wall is the kitchen garden with hot-houses and glasshouses.

Canal Garden with reeds. This may be a later view, as foliage is denser.

New Landing Stage. Steps behind the kiosk lead to the boats.

Boat House. This is below the railings and kiosk in the picture above.

The Lake, a romantic view.

ROUNDHAY PARK, LANDING STAGE, LEEDS.

Waterloo Lake. East and south of the mansion extra land was acquired around 1815 and a dam built, the valley widened and deepened in order to make this, the larger of the two lakes. It was believed to have been the work of ex-soldiers, redundant after the Napoleonic Wars.

The Upper Lake, *c*. 1908. This is just east of the mansion opposite the main entrance to the house, and is fed by a stream.

The Upper Lake. Edwardian families enjoy the park.

The Waterfall, *c*. 1911. This dramatic 60ft fall crossed by a rustic bridge pours over the sheer wall of the dam at the south end of Waterloo Lake.

Near the Gorge, *c*. 1909.

The Hermitage, *c.* 1911. At the north-east end of the Upper Lake the rustic building of rough boulders was formerly a summerhouse with a boathouse below. At the north end of Waterloo Lake the Old Castle was a mock castle or summerhouse, originally for light meals.

Silver Birches, *c.* 1907.

THE BAND-STAND, ROUNDHAY PARK, LEEDS.

Band Stand, *c*. 1911. Sited below the mansion, it is also near the lake. (see page 88)

Edwardian families listen to the band, sitting on the slope below the mansion.

Potternewton Hall, *c*. 1911. An early nineteenth-century mansion due north of the city at Harehills Lane, Chapel Allerton, this was the home of George Nussey, a dyer, and his wife. An O. Nussey Esquire, JP, was the first chairman of the Leeds Royal Exchange. The mansion became a special school.

Potternewton Park *c*. 1910. The formal landscaping down steps past urns to a circular garden and beyond is similar to that at Roundhay. By 1904, Potternewton Park had become one of Leeds Corporation's numerous municipal parks.

Armley House. This formerly modest house built in 1781 was bought in 1804 by Benjamin Gott, a Leeds merchant whose wealth came from his pioneering factories Bean Ing and Burley woollen mills. Sir Robert Smirke converted Gott's House into a splendid classical villa and Humphrey Repton landscaped the grounds which overlook the Aire valley. Gott's Bean Ing Mill in Wellington Street is now Leeds' Industrial Heritage Museum and his mansion and grounds a golf club.

Armley Park, c. 1907. One of Leeds' numerous small public parks, it is across the road from the famous HM prison, the castellated Armley Gaol of 1847 and 1857. Leeds acquired Bramley Park in 1870, part of Holbeck Moor in 1878 and Hunslet Moor in 1879.

Woodhouse Moor Gardens Entrance, *c.* 1904. The ancient common grazing grounds of the old village and new medieval town of Leeds became a public park in 1840. Popularly known as the 'Lung of Leeds' it was there that crowds escaped to from the smoky, polluted air of the industrial town.

Adam and Eve Gardens, Woodhouse Moor, *c.* 1907. The formal garden was presumably named after the classical girl and boy statues.

Adam and Eve Gardens, Woodhouse Moor. Edwardian visitors walk near the entrance lodge. It was to various locations in the park that statues from Victoria Square were removed.

The Drinking Fountain, Woodhouse Moor. Public drinking fountains were popular provisions during the Victorian temperance era. Diagonal asphalted paths intersected at this elegant stone fountain surmounted by a clock turret with four dials. The clocks, surely Potts' clocks, were the gift of Councillor Adam Brown.

The Avenue, Woodhouse Moor. Edwardian ladies are sitting and strolling in the shade.

Sunny afternoon on Woodhouse Moor, c. 1907.

The children's corner, Woodhouse Moor, *c.* 1906. Note the spindly-wheeled prams and another clock tower.

Bandstand Arena, Woodhouse Moor, *c.* 1904. A broad walk leads from the clock fountain, distant right, to the bandstand.

Woodhouse Ridge, *c*. 1907. Leeds Corporation acquired this in 1876. Woodhouse Cliff stands above and behind. These ridges are the rugged outcrops of the Millstone Grit series.

Woodhouse Ridge and Bandstand, *c*. 1918. The date-stamp says: 'BUY NATIONAL WAR BONDS NOW'.

The Ridge, Meanwood, c. 1912. In north Leeds, it overlooks the Adel Beck valley, now followed by the recreational Dales Way footpath.

Meanwood Woods, c. 1911. These are due north of the city near Adel.

Cross Flatt Park, Beeston. The aviary was a popular attraction in this built-up area near the Dewsbury Road.

Park Mansion Terrace, Dewsbury, c. 1908. Still in the built-up area around Leeds, a visit to the park mansion museum, temple folly, lake and garden made a pleasant change.

Ten
Events & Occasions

Inauguration of Statuary, City Square, 1903. On 16 September Colonel T. Walter Harding DL JP of Tower Works pin factory gifted the Black Prince statue and the eight lamp-bearing maidens Morn and Even to the City Council. (see page 23 and 73)

Lower Briggate, the Royal visit, 7 July 1908. King Edward VII and Queen Alexandra were greeted by thousands of schoolchildren.

King Edward the Peacemaker.

The Royal open carriage in the city.

The Illuminated Tram. ER was for Edwardus Rex and the other end had AR for Alexandra Regina. The side said 'Welcome to our King and Queen'. The tram toured the city centre and 3,000 electric lights were used to illuminate it.

The Welcome Arch, City Square, during the
Royal visit.

Unveiling the Queen Victoria Memorial
Statue, 1905. It stood in front of the Town
Hall steps until Victoria Square was
reorganised. She had opened the new Town
Hall in 1853, after being greeted by
thousands of schoolchildren at Woodhouse
Moor on her way into Leeds.

Proclamation Day for the new King and Queen, George V and Queen Mary, May 10, 1910, at the Town Hall steps.

The illuminated tram on Coronation Day, June 22, 1911.

The West Yorkshire Regiment during the First World War, 1914-1918. More specifically, the 3rd platoon Divisional Cyclists Corps in camp at Derby, 1915 who served as messengers. My father, Pte John Taylor, remembered washing up for ninety people there.

Wounded Soldiers. In September 1915 a hundred were entertained to tea and games by the Committees of the Headingley Grounds Athletic Association.

Harry Taylor DCM. A 1914 volunteer and a Pioneer, he was killed in action at Verchain in the battle for Valenciennes during the 'Final Advance to Victory'. The cap badge of the West Yorkshire Regiment (The Prince of Wales's Own) bore the white horse of Hanover as presented by George III.

A temporary grave marker. In the battle for Valenciennes 1-2 November 1918, 'plastered with shells, the 21st Yorkshire, the Pioneers, were as usual hard at work on the roads during the battle keeping routes open for the fighting troops who depended on their efforts'. Harry already knew that his wife had died in the 1918 'flu pandemic and their young only child of diphtheria.

Verchain British Cemetry. This is a corner of France that is forever Yorkshire.

Rue d'Arras, near Valenciennes, 1918/19.

Leeds War Memorial. A remembrance service for 'Our Glorious Dead' is held each year on Armistice Day. This cenotaph by H.C. Fahr on an island site in City Square was moved in 1937 to a Garden of Rest in front of the Art Gallery and Municipal Building next to the Town Hall.

Great Fire in Leeds. This raged on 25 July 1906. Note the dislodged hammer-dressed setts.

Leeds Association of Girl's Clubs. They won the Challenge Shield for singing in 1909.

Group of visitors to Roundhay Park, June, 1925. They are wearing an assortment of typical 1920s clothing.

Eleven
Leeds Connections

A great day out or a grand tour?

The Old Sulphur Well. The postcard message reads: 'This is where we get our sulphur water every day. The pump is on the outside and you are just allowed a quart at a time. The seventeenth century wells, The Tewit and the St John's, were in High Harrogate on the Stray. Low Harrogate developed later as the main spa. The Old Sulphur Well became the Royal Pump Room in 1842, itself later extended and now a museum. The water from the outside tap is still free!

Crescent Gardens and Royal Baths, c. 1907. The latter were built in Low Harrogate in 1897 and specialised in water-based treatments including Turkish Baths. They had assembly rooms, and concert and meeting rooms.

The Kursaal, Low Harrogate. Before the First World War this theatre and concert hall at the foot of Parliament Street was The Kursaal. After the war it was renamed The Royal Hall, as less Germanic and reflecting the prestigious clientele of the spa.

Low Harrogate Gardens, *c.* 1907. Overlooked by the Prospect Hotel, the gardens led down to the Royal Pump Room, the Valley Gardens and the Hospital. Foreign royalty visited, and HM Queen Mary patronised the antique shops. The annual Flower Show became a great attraction for visitors.

Knaresborough: Surprise view. Boating on the river Nidd and waterside cafes near the railway viaduct and Castle Crag were popular with visitors. Both Harrogate and Knaresborough became residential and retirement places for wealthy Leeds businessmen.

Knaresborough Market Place. Stalls around the Market Cross were a popular attraction, as were the ancient chemist's shop and the ruined fourteenth-century castle in its park on the crag. A Wednesday market charter was granted in 1310 although the market had existed a century earlier.

Knaresborough High Street. Separate from the Market Place, the street is little changed apart from its shop fronts and its volume and type of traffic. Mother Shipton's Cave and petrifying well, where the High Street bridges the Nidd, have long remained popular.

The Grove, Ilkley. The small town with pavement verandahs flourished as a residential outpost for Leeds and Bradford commuters. With nearby spa wells and healthy air on Ilkley Moor it also flourished as 'The Malvern of the North' with two large hydropathic hotels, Ben Rhydding, built in 1844, and Wells House, built in 1858, (see page 44). It had at least seven other similar establishments or convalescent homes. Heathcote was a Lutyens house 1906.

Industrial Hall, Bradford Exhibition, 1904. This was opened by the Prince and Princess of Wales. Bradford and Halifax had overtaken Leeds in textiles and Leeds had diversified.

The Municipal Procession entering the Exhibition Grounds. The postcard is by Rosemont, Leeds, but no other clues except dating.

Cartwright Memorial Hall, c. 1908. Samuel Cunliffe-Lister, first Baron Masham, himself a prolific inventor and textile manufacturer presented his Manningham Old Hall and Park to Bradford Corporation. In 1898, it was demolished to build this art gallery and museum Memorial Hall to Edward Cartwright (1743-1823) who invented a power loom and a wool combing machine.

Conduit Court, Skipton Castle. On a crag above the Aire, the castle, begun in Norman times, is mainly the work of the Cliffords from the fourteenth to the seventeenth century. Visitors are impressed by the mighty bastions of the gatehouse which faces the market town. Picturesque Conduit Court has the outer stairway to the Great Hall, left. Lady Anne Clifford was a prolific restorer.

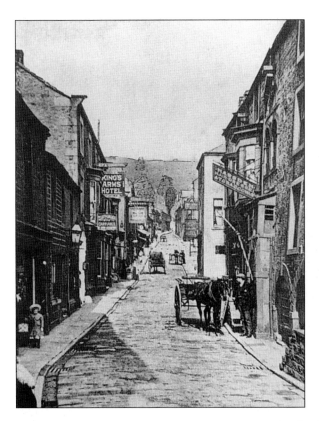

High Street, Pateley Bridge. This quaint street is still little changed but even now takes modern coaches down to the ancient bridging point of the Nidd. The tiny market town was a focus for the lead miners of Greenhow Hill across the river and for visitors to Brimham Rocks.

The Idol Stone, Brimham Rocks. The massive grits of Brimham Moor and Plumpton Rocks in Airedale were wind-eroded and sand-blasted, especially in post-glacial times when the ground was bare. Differing resistance yielded fantastic shapes given romantic names like Lovers' Leap. Famed from the eighteenth century, they were easily reached from the emerging Leeds conurbation.

York Minster from the City Walls, *c.* 1904. York became an ever popular day-trip destination as railways and motorised transport developed. Its Minster, Abbey, Roman remains, castle museums and shops drew visitors not only from Leeds and the West Riding, but from far and wide.

Church Parade, Scarborough, *c.* 1905. It was customary to walk on the South Cliff promenade on Sundays. The sender of this postcard writes: 'This is a most delightful place. Yesterday was Church Parade. You will see the Fashions on the other side. The people Promenade past the house where we are staying.' Cuthbert Brodrick's Grand Hotel is a landmark. (See page 124)

South Bay, Scarborough. 'Leeds-on-Sea' was a nickname for Scarborough. It was not only a day-tripping place and holiday destination but an ambition to retire to Scarborough when working life was over. Again Cuthbert Brodrick's Grand Hotel stands proud, a reminder of home.

Station Square, Ravenscar. In Edwardian times an ambitious plan to create a new resort beside the coastal railway at Robin Hood's Bay flopped, despite free trips from Leeds to tempt possible purchasers. An empty grid of unmade roads, a would-be Marine Esplanade and just a few scattered houses are all that remain above the 600ft drop to a pebbled seashore.

Twelve

Return to Leeds

The Black Prince and Kirkstall Abbey.

Nine Views of Leeds, *c.* 1918.

126

Statue of the Black Prince, *c.* 1905.

Roundhay Park by Moonlight, *c.* 1903.

Acknowledgements

My sincere thanks go to those who have helped in the preparation of this album of old photographs, either with information or with permission to copy and include items in their care. I have taken advice on dating and copyright.

The book is based mainly on my own collection of Edwardian postcards and I thank Alan Suddes, D.C. Geall and numerous traders at collectors' fairs and antique shops over the years. Photographs from my own inherited family albums have been included.

I also thank Darlington Borough Library Lending, Reference and Local Studies Departments for obtaining books specially and for permission to copy and use pictures in their collections.

The following have also provided help, information or pictures: Kenneth H. Chapman, Gwen M. Chapman, Timothy J. Chapman, Marie-Louise Blacow, Mike Hein-Hartmann, the late Cassy M. Harker, Roy Bradley, Richard Pepper, Gordon L. Hollis, Alan Gill, M. Campbell Cole, Pudsey Civic Society and Calverley Branch Library.

Of reference books, as ever, Nikolaus Pevsner's *Yorkshire West Riding* is basic. J S Fletcher's *The Story of the English Towns: Leeds*, (1919) and A.C. Price's *Leeds and its Neighbourhood*, (1909), have been very useful. Everard Wyrall's *The West Yorkshire Regiment in the War 1914-1918*, Vol. II, helped to elucidate the final days of the First World War for the Uncle Harry I was never to know. Above all I would recommend, congratulate and give extra thanks for two monumental and scholarly works: Steven Burt and Kevin Grady: *The Illustrated History of Leeds*, (1994) and Derek Linstrum *Towers and Colonnades - The Architecture of Cuthbert Brodrick*, (1999), which have greatly expanded my knowledge and understanding of Leeds and its neighbourhood.